D1283837

THE EAST INDIA COMPANY
BOOK OF
SPICES

ANTONY WILD

THE EAST INDIA COMPANY
BOOK OF
SPICES

ANTONY WILD

HarperCollins*Publishers*

First published in 1995 by
HarperCollins*Publishers*, London

Text © Antony Victor Wild 1995

Antony Wild asserts the moral right to
be identified as the author of this work

Editorial Director: Polly Powell
Editor: Lisa Eaton
Designer: Rachel Smyth
Picture Researcher: Lisa Eaton

The publishers and author would like to thank Amina Ricciardi,
Drew Smith and Robert Baldwin.

**A catalogue record for this book is
available from the British Library**

ISBN 0 00 412775 7

Colour reproduction by Colourscan, Singapore
Printed and bound in Spain
by Artes Graficas Toledo, S.A.
D.L.TO: 821-1995

Contents

The East India Company

The Armorial Bearings of the Company of Merchants of London trading into the East Indies granted by Garter and Clarenceux Kings of Arms in 1600, and as borne and used until 1709

*F*ounded by the Royal Charter of Queen Elizabeth I in 1600, the East India Company was the single most powerful economic force that the world has ever seen. Its influence reached out to all continents, and the consequences of its actions, both great and small, are the very fabric of history. The Company created British India; founded Hong Kong and Singapore; caused the Boston Tea Party; employed Captain Kidd to combat piracy; held Napoleon captive; and made the fortune of Elihu Yale who founded his famous university with the proceeds.

The Stars and Stripes was inspired by its flag, its shipyards provided the model for St Petersburg, its London chapel set the pattern for New England churches, its administration still forms the basis of Indian bureaucracy, and its corporate structure was the earliest example of a joint stock company. It introduced tea to Britain and India, woollens to Japan, chintzes to America, spices to the West Indies, opium to China, porcelain to Russia, and polo to Persia. It had its own armies, navies, currencies, and territories as diverse as the tiny Spice Island, Pulo Run – which was later exchanged for

Manhattan – to the 'Jewel in the Crown', India itself. As *The Times* newspaper reported in 1874 when the Company was finally absorbed by the Crown: 'It is just as well to record that it accomplished a work such as in the whole history of the human race no other Company ever attempted and, as such, is ever likely to attempt in the years to come.'

East India House

The Story of Spices

Spice and the ancient world

*T*hroughout history spices have been enormously influential in political, social and economic developments the world over. In nearly all ancient civilizations they were considered rare and valuable, prized for their preservative, medicinal and aromatic qualities.

In the West, spices were not used in cooking until the early days of the Roman Empire, although their first recorded culinary use came in ancient religious texts from around 6000 BC, called the *Hindu Vedas*. The *Ramayana*, the epic Sanskrit poem, refers to the use of spices in flavouring pilaf rice. The Babylonians, Assyrians and ancient Egyptians all used incense and holy oils infused with

Street market in Cairo, early 19th century

What is a spice?

The word spice is derived from the Latin species, *meaning a commodity of special value and distinction. A spice is usually defined as a strongly flavoured aromatic vegetable substance, obtained from the root, bark, flower or seed of a tropical plant. Nearly all known spices, with the exception of vanilla, allspice and capsicum (chilli peppers), are of oriental origin. Some spices, like frankincense and myrrh, for example, are valued purely for their aroma.*

Cinnamon and balsam, 12th century Arabic manuscript

The Emperor of China's Gardens, Peking

spices in their religious rituals, both medicinally and for the embalming of bodies. The Old Testament suggests that King Solomon's great wealth was partly due to the spice trade, and that the Queen of Sheba ruled over a section of the Incense Route through southern Arabia to the Mediterranean Sea. Alexander the Great's conquests took him as far as the Indus River, helping to open up the ancient Silk Route from China across the 'Roof of the World' to the West. Alexandria, the port he founded near the mouth of the Nile in 332 BC, became one of the main trading centres for the spice trade.

The Arab world, which already controlled both the Silk Route and the Incense Route for spices coming from the East, also tried to conceal from the Romans the origins of the Cinnamon Route. Herodotus, the Roman historian, reports that cinnamon was believed to come from the high limestone cliffs of Ethiopia, guarded by gigantic birds who used it to build their nests. Its true origins remained a mystery, and the Arab monopoly was protected until the 4th century AD when the Romans discovered cinnamon on the island of Ceylon (now Sri Lanka). In reality, cinnamon from China had been bartered for cloves from Indonesia, which were highly valued at the Chinese court. This cinnamon was then transported on outrigger canoes from Indonesia to the east coast of Africa in a daring voyage across the Indian Ocean. There it was bought by Arab traders who either took it overland up the Nile valley to Egypt, or traded it from the Red Sea ports of what is now Somalia.

An unfortunate antidote

One of the many uses of spices in ancient times was as an antidote to poisoning. This was a constant threat to leaders at the time, and the reason why so many employed food tasters. In 80 BC Crateueas, physician to Mithridates the Great, King of Pontus, devised an antidote made up of all the known spices of the day. Known as Mithridatium, it contained 36 spices ground up together and mixed with honey and wine. This proved to be so effective that, in an unforeseen twist of fate, the unfortunate Mithridates was unable to poison himself when trying to avoid capture by the Roman Emperor Pompey.

A bazaar in the Near East, 19th century

Guests being served with a spice dish, Crisso, Greece, c. 1803

Through their eastern empire the Romans came to domi-
nate much of the spice trade. Indeed the recipes of the ancient
Roman cookery writer, Apicius the Epicure, feature most of
the spices in common use today. Greek and Roman traders

Death by saffron

*Spices were held in high regard in medieval times, and none more
so than saffron, the most rare and valuable of all. Penalties for
adulteration were high: in 1456 Hans Kolbele of Nuremberg
was buried alive in the impure saffron he had been selling.*

Recipe for Spice Perfume

Mix together 3 chopped bay leaves, ½oz (15g) of bruised cloves, 2 cups of wine vinegar and 2 cups of rosewater, and bring to the boil. As it reduces, add water. When thoroughly infused, strain and place in a sealed jar for several weeks before using.

---

alike plied their trade in the Middle East and on the Indian coast of Malabar, until the fall of Rome in the 5th century AD, and Alexandria in 641 AD, ushered in the Dark Ages. For the next five centuries, until the Crusades, the entire spice trade fell under Arab control and spices became extremely rare.

The Spice Route was eventually reopened by the states of Venice and Genoa trading with the Near East, which brought about an increase in the use of spices in medieval times. In fact, the plagues ravaging Europe at this time were attributed to rats that had escaped from spice ships. Ironically, spices were used at this time in 'nosegays' – bunches of spices and dried flowers held in front of the nose to purify the air for breathing in plague areas.

The famous Lea & Perrins Worcestershire Sauce was formulated by a chemist in Worcester to the recipe of an ex-East India Company officer. It is a mixture of anchovies, garlic and raw chilli peppers. The original recipe included soy sauce, but this was dropped in the Second World War, and has never been reintroduced.

Spice seller at the bazaar, Constantinople, 1858

The spice trade

During the period of Arab domination of the spice trade, the markets of the Near East were the scene of feverish trading. The spice markets of Smyrna, Aleppo and Constantinople rose to fame at this time. The ancient port of Alexandria remained a major force in this trade as well, but eventually all succumbed to the ability of Western nations to bypass the Arab monopoly of the spice trade and deal direct with the source.

In the late 15th century the Portuguese, inspired by Henry the Navigator, found their way to India, the Far East and the Spice Islands – a small group of islands between New Guinea

The clove island of Ternate, 1724

Vasco da Gama

and the Philippines, where the only supply of cloves and nutmeg grew. Their discoveries were made possible by the daring exploits of Bartolomeu Dias, the first Westerner to round the Cape of Good Hope, and more significantly of Vasco da Gama, who made the first successful sea voyage direct to India. His well-equipped and meticulously planned voyage was backed by King Manuel I of Portugal, eager to expand Christian trade in the East. Once they had established themselves there, the Portuguese were quick to build a trading network in the East, reaching as far as China and the then virtually unknown Japan, and encompassing many of the important trading centres for spices.

Once the Portuguese acquired the strategic port of Hormuz, the Arab stranglehold over the spice trade was irrevocably broken, and Lisbon became the prime spice port.

'Awake; O North wind; and come, thou South;
Blow upon my garden, that the spices thereof may flow out'
The Bible – The Song of Solomon

The Dutch controlled the northern European spice trade, from Lisbon through to Antwerp.

One opportunity that eluded the Portuguese was to sponsor Christopher Columbus's voyage westwards to Japan. Although he failed to find an alternative route to the East, Columbus sailed with the support of the Spanish and discovered the New World, where he became the first Westerner to experience the burning, biting flavour of chillies, now so much a part of the spice repertoire.

Such a tight grip on so crucial a commodity as spices made the Portuguese a prime target for the trading ambitions of both Holland and England. Maps stolen from the

Spice plants and trees of the East Indies, c. 1576

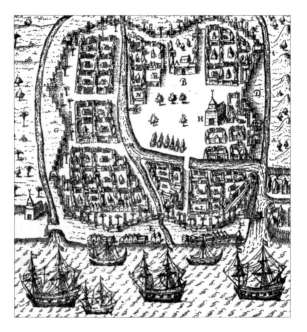

Dutch ships at anchor in Bantam, Java, 1596

Portuguese Archbishop of Goa in India, detailing navigation routes and the locations of the Spice Islands, added further impetus. In 1600 a group of London merchants obtained the Queen's Royal Charter to form the East India Company, in order to compete in this lucrative trade. The Dutch, however, had acted more quickly and had already taken advantage of the problems of the newly united Portugal and Spain to force out the Portuguese from many of the Spice Islands.

By the time the East India Company arrived they found the Dutch both well established and armed. They were forced to trade in the surrounding islands, but even as far away as Java they still had to trade alongside the well-organized Dutch. Although cloves and nutmegs remained difficult to obtain, the Company's attempts to secure pepper proved more successful. The price dropped on the London market and the term 'peppercorn rent', describing a rent lower than the usual rate, dates from this period.

Recipe for Spiced Bread

Cream 6oz (175g) of butter and 3oz (75g) of vanilla sugar together in a bowl until pale. Beat in 2 eggs, one at a time. Add 2oz (50g) of raisins, 2oz (50g) of chopped almonds, 2oz (50g) of chopped candied orange peel together with 1 teaspoon of anise seeds, 1 teaspoon of ground cinnamon and ½ teaspoon of ground cloves and stir. Sift 10oz (300g) of strong white flour and 2 teaspoons of baking powder together. Add half of this to the mixture, mixing thoroughly. Add the rest of the flour, and a little milk if the dough is too dry. Knead until firm and divide into two. Place each one in a 1lb (500g) greased bread tin. Bake in a preheated oven for 40 minutes at Gas 4 (350°F, 180°C).

In the 16th century, the Portuguese had introduced chilli peppers from South America to their Indian colonies. Before this time chillies were unknown in Indian cuisine. Europeans quickly became accustomed to the richly spiced foods of India through banquets given by Indian princes for their European counterparts, and spices for everyday cookery were sold on the streets of most Indian cities. Similarly, in the late 18th century, the East India Company began to experiment with planting spices from one country in another, using its network of Botanical Gardens to propagate the seeds. This is why pepper, cloves, nutmeg and cinnamon can be found in the West Indies today, where they have helped to create the distinctive Cajun cookery.

Banquet of spiced foods and sweetmeats, India, c. 1814

The first significant break in the Spice Islands' monopoly in nutmeg and cloves was achieved by the administrator of Mauritius, Pierre Poivre. Poivre obtained seeds of both these plants for his island, and this transplanting then spread to the Seychelles, Réunion, Zanzibar and the West Indies. The only popular spice plant which has failed to be successfully cultivated elsewhere is allspice, which is still confined to the West Indies.

European competition over the Spice Islands continued until Sir Stamford Raffles founded Singapore in 1819, giving the East India Company a secure base for their Far East spice trade. The late 18th century also saw

Bust of Sir Stamford Raffles

A royal favourite

The one tiny nutmeg-producing Spice Island held by the Company in the King's name became such a source of pride to James I that he styled himself: 'King of England, Scotland, Ireland, France … and Puloroon.' Eventually the island was ceded to the Dutch under the Treaty of Breda in 1667, in exchange for a slightly better-known island – Manhattan.

Inspecting cinnamon at the docks before auction, 1903

a new player enter the spice trade, with the New England ports of America competing fiercely with the Dutch and English, particularly for cargoes of pepper. Later the trade concentrated in New York, which still deals with most of the spices entering the United States, followed by Baltimore and San Francisco.

Spices today

As a result of the worldwide spread of spices, no one country has been able to keep a monopoly of any particular plant. Never before has there been such an abundance of spices at affordable prices. The United States is the chief importer of spices, followed by Germany, Japan and France. The trade is worth around £1 billion ($1.5 billion) a year, representing some 350,000 tonnes (350 million kilos) of spices. Although this may seem a substantial quantity, in comparison to other cash crops, the quantities of spices are relatively insignificant – the global coffee market, for example, is about ten times larger by weight. However, like other cash crops, spices contribute greatly to the balance of payments of the tropical developing countries where they are grown. To this day black pepper has remained the most widely used spice, followed by capsicums (chillies) and cardamom. The use of spices varies enormously by country and by cuisine. Cardamom, for example,

Drying cloves in Sumatra

Sorting red pepper in Japan, 1922

is popular in Arab countries, where it is frequently added to coffee, while in other countries juniper is used for the flavouring of gin, and vanilla for chocolate and ice cream. In Indonesia cloves are very popular for use in *kretek* cigarettes.

Today India is the principal producer of spices for the world market, exporting 70,000 tonnes (70 million kilos) a year, or about 20 per cent of the global trade – mainly pepper, chillies, turmeric, ginger and large quantities of curry powder. Indonesia, the second largest producer, still specializes in the traditional cloves, nutmeg and pepper, but now also produces vanilla and ginger. Other major producers include Brazil, Madagascar and Malaysia. The food industry's hunger for spices has led to the development of oleoresins – highly concentrated forms of spices which are easier to handle for bulk users. Many spice-producing countries, therefore, now have oleoresin manufacturing plants.

For reasons of cost and quality control, most spices are exported in bulk. Whether fresh or dried, they are cleaned, graded and packed in the importing country by specialist companies. They are then usually sold under a particular manufacturer's brand name, as the consumer or industrial user is rarely sufficiently discerning to differentiate between a spice from one origin or another. They rely instead on the expertise of the chosen supplier to make the right choice.

Although fresh spices preserve the best flavour, many consumer markets use them dried or even ready-ground, and fresh spices are often difficult to find. While pre-ground spices remove the need for such traditional implements as nutmeg graters, pepper grinders and clove infusers, some of their flavour can be lost in the process.

*19th century silver
nutmeg graters*

How spices work

Recent research in the United States may provide an answer as to why something so hot to taste as certain spices can be so popular. It seems that the burning sensation induced by many of the hotter spices is a response to pain of nerve endings in the tongue. This may trigger the release of endorphins, the body's own natural painkillers, which then give rise to pleasurable, even euphoric sensations.

Recipe for Spiced Beef

Mix together 2oz (50g) of cardamom, 1oz (25g) of crystallized ginger, 2oz (50g) of juniper berries, 2oz (50g) of black and white pepper, 5 cloves and 8oz (250g) of red raisins and grind coarsely. Mix in 2oz (50g) of coarse sea salt and place in a deep earthenware dish with a lid. Roll a large silverside of beef in the mixture, making sure that all the surface meat and fat is covered. Press in the remaining spices by hand so that the covering is as thick as possible. Cover and refrigerate for a week to ten days, turning and reapplying the spices daily. Remove from the dish, wipe clean of all spices, and roast in a very low oven.

Allspice

*Capsicum
(chilli pepper)*

Cardamom

Spices of the World

Lemon grass

Nutmeg and mace

Pepper

Cinnamon
and cassia

Cloves

Coriander

Cumin

Frankincense
and myrrh

Ginger

Saffron

Turmeric

Vanilla

Allspice

The history of allspice

First discovered in Mexico by early Spanish explorers,
allspice was mistaken for pepper and named 'pimiento',
which was later anglicized to 'pimento'. Its heady
combination of the flavours of cloves, cinnamon, nutmeg and
pepper (which led to its French name *quatre épices* – four spices)
gained in popularity, but the plant proved difficult to
cultivate in other tropical regions. The main centre for
production is Jamaica, where natural forest paths consisting
mainly of allspice trees are known as 'Pimento Walks'. At the
turn of the century a sudden fashion for pimento-wood
handles for umbrellas and walking sticks threatened
temporarily to reduce the supply of allspice.

The allspice plant

An evergreen tropical tree of the myrtle family, *Pimenta dioica*
can reach a height of 30 feet (9 metres), producing berries
the size of small peas. These are harvested while they are a
mature green colour, rather than a ripe purple, and are then
dried in the sun or in kilns, turning red-brown. An early

botanist described how in a Jamaican Pimento Walk: 'The friction of the leaves and small branches even in a gentle breeze diffuses a most exhilarating scent.'

How allspice is used

Allspice has excellent preservative qualities, and is a favourite of the food industry. Tomato ketchups and sauces, canned meat and, particularly, pickled fruit and vegetables all contain allspice. The main users are the Scandinavian countries, using allspice to pickle raw herrings. Giving a rich warm flavour to cakes, jams, pies, and stewed fruits, it is also used in Britain in traditional mincemeat and Christmas pudding. Its heady aromas make it a popular ingredient of men's scents, and, on a more practical level, it was used by Napoleon's troops inside their boots to keep their feet warm on the retreat from Moscow.

Capsicum

The history of capsicum

A native of Peru, the capsicum (or chilli pepper) was widely cultivated in Central and South America before the arrival of Europeans, and was well-known to the Mayans and Aztecs, who used it to flavour cocoa. Introduced to Europe in the 16th century by the Spanish, it was then transplanted by the Portuguese to India, where it now forms an indispensable part of the cuisine. There are an enormous variety of capsicums, ranging from the sweet bell peppers used in salads, to the tiny, very hot varieties such as bird's eye chilli.

The capsicum plant

There are two varieties of capsicum plant: *Capsicum annuum*, a tropical evergreen bush which grows to a height of about 3 feet (1 metre) and produces the rounded varieties of fruit, and *Capsicum frutescens*, which grows to a height of 6½ feet (2 metres) and produces the more pointed, hotter peppers. Different varieties of capsicums are now grown all over the world, although in cooler climates such as Europe they have to be kept under glass. They are sold fresh, dried or powdered according to region and convention. Cayenne pepper, for example, is a very powerful blend of powdered red chillies. Paprika is a milder version of the same, made without the seeds, used in the preparation of Hungarian goulash. Tabasco sauce is a mixture of hot chillies and vinegar.

How capsicum is used

Fresh chilli peppers should be smooth and unwrinkled. Much of the heat is contained in the seeds and, if required, these can be removed by slicing the chilli lengthwise and teasing them out with the point of a knife. Always be careful after handling chillies as your hands will burn whatever sensitive areas you touch, especially the·eyes. While too many chillies can actually burn the mouth or the stomach lining, they are a useful aid to the digestion of starchy foods like rice or pasta.

Cardamom

The history of cardamom

Since ancient times cardamom has been known to the Indians as 'The Queen of the Spices'. In traditional Indian Ayurvedic medicine cardamom was used for the treatment of skin disorders and as a cure for coughing. Introduced gradually to the West through the early spice traders, it soon became one of the most prized spices of ancient Rome, and an especial favourite of Apicius the Epicure. An important flavouring for food, it was also valued as a breath freshener, and used by the ancient Egyptians as a tooth whitener.

The cardamom plant

Elletaria cardamomum is a native of the tropical forests of southern India, where it thrives at a steady temperature of 73°F (23°C). This perennial bush grows to a height of about 10 feet (3 metres), and produces pods at intervals during the summer. These must be harvested before they split open on the plant and are then laid out in the sun to dry. The plant is now also grown in Sri Lanka, Guatemala, Vietnam and Tanzania, but is difficult to cultivate and so still commands high prices on the world market. As a result, inferior varieties of cardamom pods are sometimes sold. These have a much rougher appearance.

How cardamom is used

The flavour of cardamom is contained in the tiny hard seeds inside the pods. It has a mellow lemon and camphor smell, which lends itself equally to sweet or savoury dishes. One of the main ingredients of garam masala, the classic Indian spice mixture, cardamom also features in pilaf dishes. It is particularly popular in Arab countries, where it is commonly infused with coffee, or even green tea. In Scandinavia it is popular in spiced breads and pastries. A further use is for neutralizing the smell of garlic.

Cinnamon and Cassia

The history of cinammon and cassia

The spice which originally came to the West from China via Indonesia on the Cinnamon Route was in fact cassia. Although a close relative of cinnamon, cassia is much coarser in appearance and flavour. Real cinnamon came originally from Ceylon, and was first recorded in 1275 in a work by the Arab writer Kazwini. The Portuguese, the Dutch and then finally the East India Company all cultivated cinnamon in Ceylon. Indeed they were so successful that they sometimes flooded the world market and had to destroy the crop.

The cinnamon and cassia plants

Cassia is still produced predominantly in China, while the cultivation of the more popular cinnamon has spread from Ceylon to India, the Seychelles, Brazil and Jamaica. Real cinnamon, *Cinnamomum zeylanicum*, is a tropical evergreen tree which grows to a height of some 33 feet (10 metres). The spice itself comes from the inner bark of the tree, which is why it is sometimes found in quills or dried tubes of the bark. It is harvested during the rainy season, the coarser outer layers of the bark gradually cropped until the fine inner bark is revealed. The quills are then slowly dried in the shade to preserve their shape. Ground cinnamon is paler in colour than ground cassia.

How cinnamon and cassia are used

Cassia is still an essential ingredient of Chinese cuisine. Although less aromatic than real cinnamon, it has a more intense flavour, and is better suited to savoury dishes than sweet. Cinnamon is one of the prime ingredients of garam masala, and is also found in Indian curds. The Arabs use it with rice and it is particularly suited to lamb. In European cookery cinnamon is used primarily in fruit compôtes, cakes and pastries. Traditionally cinnamon was the flavouring for spiced ale and wine, and is still a key ingredient in mulled wine. Cinnamon spiced tea has become increasingly popular and is used by herbalists to suppress nausea.

A spiced tea can be made by adding a little cinnamon, cloves, allspice and cardamom to black tea. Experiment until you find the proportions that suit your taste.

'Spices, which the more they are pounded, The sweeter they are.'
George Pettie on the lessons of adversity

Cloves

The history of cloves

One of the key spices of the ancient world, cloves were first recorded in use by the Chinese in the 1st century BC. The emperors of the Han Dynasty expected supplicants to approach them with a clove in their mouths to freshen the breath. Known to the Romans and in Europe through medieval times, cloves later became the object of intense competition between the Portuguese, Dutch and English as they sought to establish trade with the only known source, the Spice Islands. The Dutch dominated until 1770, when Pierre Poivre smuggled seedlings to Mauritius.

The cloves plant

Syzygium aromaticum is an evergreen tropical tree which grows to a height of about 30 feet (9 metres) and produces small, intensely aromatic pink flower buds twice a year. Buds are harvested before they open by beating the branches, and are then dried in the sun, where they turn a deep red-brown. Originally only found in the Spice Islands, cloves are now also grown in Mauritius, Madagascar, Grenada, India and

Zanzibar said to be the best source. They rate as the second most important spice in the world, although half the amount produced goes into Indonesian clove cigarettes.

How cloves are used

An important component of garam masala and pilafs, cloves are also used in pickles and Indian sweets. Their nail-like shape is ideal for studding roast and baked meats, (particularly ham), and their warm, rich flavour adds to stews and bread sauce as well as sweet dishes, particularly those containing apples. The Germans use cloves in spiced bread, and they are an essential ingredient of British mincemeat, a fruit filling. An aid to indigestion and other intestinal complaints, cloves are also well known for alleviating the pain of toothache, when a clove softened in warm honey is held against the tooth. They are also found in antiseptic toothpastes and mouthwashes.

Cloves stuck into an orange make a traditional pomander for keeping clothes smelling fresh.

Coriander

The history of coriander

Like cumin, coriander is a native plant of the eastern Mediterranean, and is mentioned in ancient Egyptian, Sanskrit and Greek writings. The Romans spread its use throughout Europe and it was well known in medieval times, when it was nicknamed 'dizzycorn' due to its narcotic effect on animals when eaten in large quantities. It was thought to be an aphrodisiac and appears in the *Thousand and One Nights*. One of the first spices to be introduced to the United States, coriander was recorded as being grown in Massachusetts in 1670.

The coriander plant

Coriandrum sativum is a hardy annual plant which resembles flat parsley. Growing to a height of around 20 inches (50 centimetres), it produces small white or pink flowers. The plant has the distinction of producing both a spice (the sun-dried seeds) and a herb (the stem leaves). The berries with the seeds must be fully ripe before harvesting, as it is only then that they develop their sweet, spicy aroma. The spice tastes sweet and hot, with a slight citrus flavour. In India the seeds are lightly roasted before use. The leaves are used fresh.

How coriander is used

Ground coriander is used in pickling, spiced meats and baking in Europe and America, and in France forms the basis of vegetable dishes *à la grecque*. It is also used in confectionery and liqueurs. The leaves are used in salads, chilled soups, and meat and stuffings, particularly in the Middle East.

In Indian cuisine the leaves are also put into the chutney which accompanies most savoury snacks, as well as a basic meat sauce, fried together with green chillis, tomatoes and onions. The ground spice is a basic ingredient of curry powder, giving both body and flavour.

*'Sugar and spice and all that's nice
That's what little girls are made of'*
Nursery rhyme by J O Halliwell

Cumin

The history of cumin

A native of the Nile valley, cumin was well known in the ancient world, appearing in the Old Testament and in Greek writings. Seeds were found in the tombs of the Pharaohs, and the Romans used cumin as we now use pepper. The Greeks defined a miser as one who counted cumin seeds, and this was the nickname of the Roman Emperor Marcus Aurelius. Popular among the Celts and Normans for spicing baked fish, it was well-established in Britain by the 15th century. Although less used now in the West, cumin has become an indispensable feature of Indian cookery.

The cumin plant

A small annual plant with a pungent aroma, *Cuminum cyminum* grows to a height of around 6 inches (15 centimetres). Today cumin is cultivated in warm climates all around the world, but can flourish as far north as Norway. The whole plant is harvested, and the small sharp-ended seeds are threshed out. In India the seeds are frequently dry-roasted before grinding, but elsewhere are used whole or ground as they are. North

Indian cookery sometimes uses 'black cumin', a more expensive variant which grows in the Vale of Kashmir and Iran.

How cumin is used

In France and Germany the seeds are sometimes used whole in bread and cakes, and in Holland and Switzerland in cheeses. An essential ingredient of chilli con carne, cumin is also used in couscous and Arabic ground lamb and beef dishes. In India it is a major ingredient of garam masala, curry powder and many pickles. Cumin is also often an ingredient in perfumes and is a flavouring for kümmel liqueur.

Recipe for Garam Masala

This classic Indian sweet spice mixture can be varied according to preference, but usually consists of some combination of the following: 3 inch (8 centimetre) stick of cinammon (broken into pieces), 2 tablespoons of coriander seeds, 1 tablespoon of cumin seeds, 1 teaspoon of whole cloves, 1 teaspoon of cardamom pods, 1 tablespoon of mace and 1 tablespoon of black peppercorns. Grind or pound all these together. Keep in an airtight container in a cool dark place. Sprinkle over the chosen dish when nearly ready.

Frankincense and Myrrh

The history of frankincense and myrrh

Frankincense and myrrh are aromatic spices and are not valued for their taste; indeed, the old Hebrew word *mur* means 'bitter'. Nonetheless in ancient times they formed part of the wider trade in spices, and were highly valued – as the Three Kings' famous gift to the new-born Jesus of 'gold, frankincense and myrrh' suggests. The ancient Greeks prized a liquid form of myrrh known as stacte, and frankincense was known in both Arab and Chinese medicine.

The frankincense and myrrh plants

Both frankincense and myrrh are gums which are exuded, either naturally or from cuts, from the bark of wild bushes. In the case of frankincense, the gum is a milky liquid from a tree of the species *Boswelia*, grown wild in Africa and Asia. This gum hardens on contact with air and turns a yellow colour. Myrrh comes from *Commiphora abyssinica*, a bush grown only in the basaltic soils of Somalia and parts of Arabia. It is a brownish yellow colour with a marked bitter taste. As the liquid gum hardens it forms into globules known as 'tears'.

How frankincense and myrrh are used

As aromatic spices, the principal use of both frankincense and myrrh has been in incense and perfumery. Myrrh was also employed by the ancient Egyptians in the embalming of bodies, and is used today as a mouthwash and an ingredient in some tooth powders.

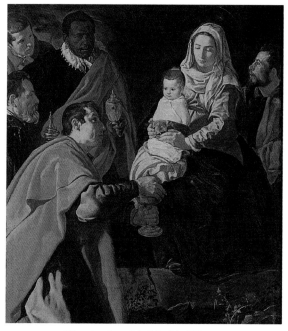

'The adoration of the Magi' by Velasquez

Ginger

The history of ginger

Ginger was familiar to the civilizations of both ancient China and India. It appeared in the writings of the philosopher Confucius in the 5th century BC, and also featured in Ayurvedic medicine for the relief of liver complaints and anaemia. Rich in vitamin C, it was eaten fresh by early Chinese mariners to ward off scurvy. Ginger was the second favourite spice of the Romans, and by the year 1000 AD was established throughout Europe. Its cultivation then spread to the West Indies, through the Spanish, and to west Africa through the Portuguese.

Recipe for Mulled Wine

Boil ¼ pint (150 ml) of water and add 1 small cinnamon quill, 1 small piece of bruised dried ginger, 8 cloves, orange peel and 3oz (75g) of white sugar to make a syrup. Then add a bottle of red wine and allow to heat, but not to boil, before serving.

The ginger plant

Zingiber officinale is a creeping plant which grows to a height of 3 feet (0.9 metres) and thrives in tropical southern Asia. The underground rhizome, or stem, is harvested after about six months if fresh or stem ginger is required, or after ten months for the more fibrous dried ginger. Fresh ginger is made by simply washing and drying the rhizome. Stem, or preserved ginger is made by soaking the rhizome in brine, boiling it and then placing it in a syrup. Dried ginger is made by boiling or peeling the rhizome before drying.

How ginger is used

Ginger is one of the most versatile spices. Greatly used in Indian and Chinese cuisines, it is also found in traditional Western recipes such as gingerbread – a favourite of Elizabeth I of England – ginger wine and ginger beer. It has a hot, biting, but sweet, woody flavour. A key ingredient of curry powder, it is also used pickled as an accompaniment to Japanese sushi. It is believed to improve circulation, aid digestion and relieve colds when made into a tea.

Gingerbread seller, 1804

Lemon grass

The history of lemon grass

Used in ancient Ayurvedic medicine, lemon grass has also
long been a staple ingredient of Southeast Asian cookery. Its
Sanskrit name was *Bhustrina*. An infusion of its leaves was used
to relieve catarrh, and the oil was employed in the treatment
of cholera. The highest quality lemon grass is still found on
the Malabar coast near the ancient spice port of Cochin, and
it is likely that early Arab and Roman traders there knew of
the plant and its extract.

The lemon grass plant

Lemon grass, *Cymbopogon citratus*, is now cultivated in
Southeast Asia, Africa and parts of Central and South
America, as well as India, where it is also known as 'Indian
Verbena'. It is a tall tropical perennial grass with a bulb,
which thrives on sandy soil in hot climates with plenty of
rain. Harvested about four months after planting, lemon
grass is used fresh, dried or powdered in cookery. There
are also many uses for the oil, which is extracted from the
plant by steaming.

How lemon grass is used

The characteristic lemon taste of lemon grass comes from its citral content, which is at its highest in the fresh plant – dried leaves and powdered versions lack flavour. The chopped stalk is used in soups and stews, but is hard to chew even after cooking, and should be pounded into a paste if it is to be eaten. It is particularly suited to fish and poultry dishes. Lemon grass oil is used in perfumes, soaps, detergents and toiletries to give a fresh lemon aroma. Although still a part of Ayurvedic medicine, lemon grass is no longer used in Western herbalism.

Indian spices and sweetmeat seller, c. 1850

Nutmeg and Mace

The history of nutmeg and mace

Similar spices derived from the same tree, nutmeg and mace
were Ayurvedic remedies for easing headaches and fevers.
They appeared comparatively late in the West, and were
used to scent the streets of Rome at the coronation of
Emperor Henry VI in 1190. When the Portuguese seized the
Spice Islands, nutmeg became so fashionable that people
wore strings of them around their necks and carried graters.
In America, enterprising tricksters forged false nutmegs out
of whittled wood and sold them – earning Connecticut the
misleading title 'The Nutmeg State'.

The nutmeg and mace plants

The nutmeg tree, *Myristica fragrans*, is a tropical maritime tree
growing up to 60 feet (18.3 metres) in height. It produces
small fruits resembling apricots which fall to the ground
when ripe. The first layers of rind crack open to reveal a
smooth, hard nut with a crimson lacy covering. The covering
is removed and dried in the sun for a few hours, paling in
colour and turning brittle – this is mace. The nut is dried

separately for as much as six weeks, by which time the kernel, which is the nutmeg, rattles around inside the smooth shell and can be removed.

How nutmeg and mace are used

Mace is less aromatic and has a slightly more refined, bitter flavour than nutmeg, and tends to be used in savouries such as sausages, fish dishes and ketchup. Nutmeg is used mainly with baked products, sweet puddings and ales. It is very popular with the Dutch, who keep nutmeg grinders handy to add it to mashed potatoes, cabbage and rice dishes. A whole nutmeg carried in the pocket is supposed to cure rheumatism, but an excess of nutmeg can cause myristicin poisoning, leading to hallucinations and even death.

Cameline, a famous French sauce of the Middle Ages, was a mixture of cinnamon, ginger, cloves, grains of paradise, mace, pepper and bread soaked in vinegar.

Pepper

The history of pepper

Pepper has long been one of the most popular spices. When the Goths threatened to sack Rome in AD 408, they demanded pepper, gold and silver as a ransom. The Portuguese monopoly on pepper led to the formation of the East India Company, after which pepper became affordable to everyone for the first time. As late as the 1800s, fortunes were still being made in Salem, on the east coast of the United States, from the control of the Sumatran pepper trade.

The pepper plant

Pepper, *Piper nigrum*, is the source of green (fresh, pickled or dehydrated), black and white peppercorns. The plant is a perennial climbing shrub native to southern India, but is now cultivated in Indonesia, Brazil and Sarawak. It can reach over 30 feet (9 metres) in height and produces small berries, which are green when they first reach maturity. These are then harvested and can be sold fresh or pickled, or are left to ferment in the sun, forming wrinkled black peppercorns. White peppercorns come from the berries which have matured to a red or yellow colour. The flesh of the berry is soaked off to expose the white peppercorn inside, which is then dried. Although when properly made in this way white pepper is of a higher quality and milder taste, the use of machines in today's processing often leaves the shrivelled skin of the black pepper only partially removed.

How pepper is used

The predominant flavour of pepper combines a pronounced pungency with an aromatic woodiness. It is one of the few spices that can be added before, during and after cooking. It has natural preservative qualities – one of the reasons why it is frequently used in sausages – and stimulates the taste buds, causing gastric secretions and helping digestion. It is best to use white pepper in white sauces, as black pepper will spoil their appearance.

'Manhood, learning, gentleness, virtue, youth
Liberality, and such like
The spice and salt that season a man'
Shakespeare – Troilus and Cressida

Quatre épices, the classic French four-spice mix for stews, is made of five parts black pepper, two parts nutmeg, and one part each of cloves and ginger.

Saffron

The history of saffron

Saffron was, and remains, the most expensive spice in the world. Originating in the Near East, it was used by the Persian Court as both a flavouring and dye, and was later adopted by the Romans. It was claimed that Nero tinted his bathwater with it. By the 10th century cultivation had spread to Spain, and thereafter to France, Germany and England, where the town of Saffron Walden became a centre of production in the 15th century. One of the few spices exported to India and China in ancient times, saffron is still much used in the traditional cuisines of these countries.

The saffron plant

Crocus sativus flowers in the autumn in warm, dry conditions. At the centre of its blue-lilac flowers lie three blood-red stigma which form the saffron 'threads' when dried. Although now cultivated throughout the Mediterranean, Iran, Kashmir, India and China, it is still extremely expensive. This is because up to a quarter of a million plants, all hand picked, are required to yield a single pound (0.45 kilo) of saffron.

How saffron is used

Saffron is a feature of those classic Mediterranean specialities, Spanish paella, French bouillabaisse and Italian risotto. It is partly used for its colour, but also for its exotic aroma and slightly bitter flavour. Saffron should be used sparingly, as too much will give an unwanted medicinal taste. Applied in Indian cookery to pilafs, biryani dishes and some sweets, it is also used in the West in cakes and breads for colour and flavour. For cooking purposes it is better to buy the 'threads' – the powder may be adulterated – and to soak them in a tiny amount of hot water, adding both to the ingredients. Saffron has many other uses, from creating the caste marks of Indian women through to flavouring chartreuse liqueur.

Turmeric

The history of turmeric

First recorded in Assyrian herbals dating back to 600 BC, turmeric was once as highly valued as ginger, but has now fallen from favour in the West. Marco Polo observed it in 1280 in Fokien, China, and remarked that it seemed to be used in the same way as saffron. In India it was originally seen as a cheap alternative to saffron, partly as a colouring agent and partly for its flavour. Nowadays, however, it forms an essential part of curry powder and many vegetarian recipes. Turmeric dye was used for the robes of Buddhist monks.

The turmeric plant

Curcuma longa is a tropical plant of the ginger family, with clusters of flowers and leaves reaching around 3 feet (1 metre) in length. Like ginger, it produces underground rhizomes, from which turmeric is derived. The rhizomes are harvested ten months after planting, boiled, peeled and then dried for ten days. They are usually sold whole to traders, but are generally ground industrially before being sold to consumers. Turmeric is bright orange when fresh, but changes to yellow in its dried form.

Marco Polo leaving Venice on his travels

How turmeric is used

Turmeric has a pungent, musky, slightly bitter flavour. In Western cookery it is used in preserves and relishes, including piccalilli. It can be put into salad dressings, and is frequently added to commercial mustards. In Indian cookery it is used with meat, fish, egg and poultry, and all curry powders. It forms the basis of marinades, and is often added to beans and lentils for colour and additional flavour. It is thought to aid digestion, and is used in the treatment of liver complaints, including jaundice.

Vanilla

The history of vanilla

Vanilla was first actively cultivated by the Aztecs, and its use for flavouring the Emperor Montezuma's chocolate was noted in 1520 by a Spanish conquistador. Its popularity spread to Europe in the 17th century when chocolate drinking became fashionable, but it was also used to scent tobacco. Its cultivation remained a monopoly of Mexico until 1841, when the technique for hand pollination was discovered and new plantings began in Java. Artificial vanilla was first produced in 1874, but, although its quality has improved substantially, it is no substitute for the subtle, sweet perfumed flavour of real vanilla.

The vanilla plant

The vanilla plant, *Vanilla planifolia*, is a tropical climbing orchid now cultivated in most of Central America, Madagascar and Réunion. The plant produces yellow-green flowers which depend on Mexican species of bee and humming bird for pollination. The vanilla pods are actually the unripe fruit, and have to undergo an elaborate and costly 'curing' process to develop the characteristic favour. The best pods turn a rich dark brown and are coated with a natural white crystal called vanillin.

How vanilla is used

Vanilla is one of the world's most popular flavours, used mainly in sweet dishes, cakes, biscuits, puddings and ice creams. It is still an essential ingredient of chocolate, and although the lower quality brands use synthetic substitutes, good chocolate should always be flavoured with natural vanilla. A vanilla pod can be used, dried and then used again a number of times. Vanilla essence is very powerful and should be used sparingly. Although vanilla was once thought to have medicinal properties – including the ability to calm hysterics – it is now only used as a flavouring agent.

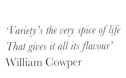

'*Variety's the very spice of life*
That gives it all its flavour'
William Cowper

Index

Picture Credits

The publisher thanks the photographers and organizations for their kind permission to reproduce the following photographs in this book: